Bereavement

by

CANON WILLIAM PURCELL

CONTENTS

MOWBRAY
LONDON & OXFORD

BEREAVEMENT

Facing up to it

Bereavement is the loss through death of a
loved person; husband, wife, son, daughter or
friend. It is a common experience: it comes to
most of us at some time or other: yet every
bereavement is unique and special to the person
concerned. Every bereavement also brings its
particular difficulties, challenges, and problems.
So every bereavement is a testing experience.
But the more we can face up to the facts of it
and come to understand some things about it,
the more able we are going to be to pass
through this difficult passage of life.

A recently widowed woman who said, of the
death of her husband, 'It's been such a shock'
was speaking the truth. It always is. She
added:'Things can never be the same again'.
she was quite right there, too, even though in
fact she was speaking out of the depths of
grief. Yet to think of the experience in this
shattered way is to make a desolation out of
something which can be both creative and
ennobling if faced with understanding.

It is true that things would never be the same
again for this woman or for any other in that
situation. Nothing could recreate the life she had
known when her husband was alive. The real

question is what she would make out of the new situation now that he was dead. That is a basic question which faces all of us as we enter into our own particular Valley of the Shadow at the death of someone dear. It cannot be answered until some of the facts about that Valley are faced.

Facing the facts

The rewards of such a facing of facts are rich indeed: for they can help not only with our own bereavements when they come; but also with those of other people. The need in this area is very great. Sorrow arising from bereavement, one of the most universal of emotional states, is at the same time one of the least understood. A lot of people seem to think of it still as a weakness, because so many people are embarrassed by tears. But after all, Christ himself wept at the grave of his friend, (John 11.35), and said 'Blessed are those who mourn, for they shall be comforted'. (Matthew 5.4). The fact is that bereavement has to be faced. Its sorrows need to be recognised: its emotions given free rein. Healing lies in expression, not in repression. After all, sorrow is as much a part of life as joy. It is the price we pay for love.

So this necessity of sorrow is one of the major facts to be faced about bereavement. The further truth is that it is, in its own way, an illness. The way in which it is often spoken of reveals this fact. Thus people speak of bereavement as a 'blow', of sorrow as a 'wound', which time may or may not 'heal'. Bereaved people are also by custom treated as though they were ill: expected to take time off work; spoken of and to in hushed tones, as though in a sick-room; relieved as far as possible of tasks and decisions.

Then eventually the 'illness' is regarded as over, and the convalescent encouraged to return to normal life, much as someone who has, for instance, broken a leg, is urged to try and walk on it again. Indeed, so close is bereavement to being an illness that it can produce physical symptoms, of which sleeplessness, or loss of weight, or even gain of weight, or anxiety states requiring drugs, including the use of tranquillizers, are but a few. A high proportion of a group of widows studied in this connection were discovered to have consulted their doctor within a few weeks of bereavement.

Emotional consequences
One writer in this field, Doctor Murray Parkes, has noted two particular consequences of bereavement: stigma and deprivation. Several women, when asked what their first reactions

had been to the loss of their husbands, gave, perhaps unconsciously, a definition of stigma. All said that they felt that they had experienced a loss of status. They were diminished in the world. And though people were kind, they were also pitying, which for the person on the receiving end, was itself belittling. Or at least they had found it so although no doubt it was kindly meant. One of those widows, indeed, found this so trying that she had been moved to pull up all her roots of old associations and to move away from the district in which she had been living.

Stigma
What is the origin of this strange phenomenon of stigma? Basically it arises from fear — the fear of death. That is why, in some primitive societies, widows have been treated as taboo, as far as possible and for a time not to be approached; but isolated in a place by themselves. In one primitive society it was the custom, for instance, that a widow could only go out at an hour of the day, usually at dusk, when she was unlikely to meet anyone! Whoever saw her was thought to die a sudden death. To prevent this she would knock with a wooden peg on the trees as she went along, warning people of her coming. It was even

believed that the trees on which she knocked would soon die. Some understanding of such strange facts as this can help us to understand not only our own bereavements, but also those of others, and therefore be all the better equipped to be of help to them.

Role change
Very deep, therefore, lie the roots from which comes stigma. So any widow who senses now the gradual withdrawal of her former friends, and a general avoidance of her company is experiencing something of this strange and ancient aversion. Sometimes it is even encouraged by the woman herself, who withdraws from company as if shrinking into a shell. That is why it is quite common to meet a bereaved person who feels an overmastering desire to be alone. Others feel a great desire to change their way of life and to undertake something entirely different from what they were doing before. This is known as a role change, the desire to become a different personality as a way of getting away from the ache of the sorrow which bereavement has caused. One of the greatest of helps which can be given by relatives and friends is love based on understanding of what the bereaved person is going through in these respects.

What then is deprivation? This means loss of someone who has been a provider, a sustainer, a companion. Bereavement bears particularly hard at this point. The consequence of deprivation is loneliness, just as the consequence of loss is grief. This loneliness which, like stigma, has deep and ancient roots in human behaviour is hard to bear. It is also likely to continue until the gaps in life left by it can be filled by other interests. This development is much to be encouraged, because the gaps of loneliness have to be filled.

But this is not always easy. Not everyone can manage it. Widowers may find it even more difficult than widows, because they are usually less able to look after themselves. And bereaved parents may find it most difficult of all, because the loss of a child presents special problems of grief, with the accompanying emotions of guilt, remorse and anger against God and man.

But always it is true that to express these griefs is vital, to accept these losses essential, because acceptance is always the way out of bitterness and back to the love of God.

Helping the bereaved

All of us want to be of help to the bereaved, as to others, whenever we can. That is why it is important to try and understand the states of mind which bereavement brings about. Obviously, because people and circumstances vary so much, there cannot be any set pattern to it. A sudden death may produce a shock to the bereaved severe enough to act as a kind of anaesthetic, so that the bereaved person may appear for a time so numbed as to be unable to express any emotion at all commensurate with the situation. Or it may be that they feel it actually wrong to show emotion, preferring rather to bottle it up. It is an odd fact about the way that we live now that we seem to find it so difficult to cope with sorrow. Thus a crying child in public is a matter for concern. But a crying grown-up is a fearful embarrassment, almost an indecency. And none of this makes it any easier to help the bereaved, or for the bereaved to help themselves.

Children and bereavement
Now this mention of the crying child raises a matter of great importance. It should never be forgotten that children are bereaved, that children have a work of mourning to do. The tendency to try to disguise from them what has happened can be cruel and damaging, so can the temptation to fall back upon such cosmetic statements as that 'Daddy has gone to Jesus'. Or that, maybe, a little sister has been 'Taken to

Heaven because God wanted her'. Hiding death from children can do great harm. They know that it has happened. They must be helped, and it is often not so difficult as it is with adults. For if a child is talked to lovingly, openly, and in terms which make sense, which should be possible for Christians who believe in the life of the world to come, the child will cope in his or her own way.

There may be a period of fear, and then of anger against the parent trying to explain matters, and then sometimes what appears to be a complete switch off back to normal interests.

Perhaps teenagers need more special help, because obviously they are more developed. The case of a girl whose older brother, whom she adored, died, is illuminating. No one spoke to her about it. She went into her grief alone. She was not even invited to the funeral. She felt cruelly excluded from a grief which the rest of the family were sharing and, though they had excluded her for the best of reasons, the results were disastrous.

It can be summed up by saying that perhaps the two greatest dangers, even maybe the two greatest sins, in the treatment of children and young people involved in the bereavement are falsity and secrecy.

What happens after bereavement

To return to adults, when there has been a period of acute anxiety and suffering accompanying a last illness there may well come a sense of relief to the survivor which for a time can over-ride sorrow. There can also be a determination not to face the fact of death. This can be so resolute as to lead to the self-deception that it has not happened. A classic instance was the reaction of Queen Victoria to the loss of her husband. The Prince Consort's rooms, by her order, were left exactly as they had been during his life. Even his shaving things were set out ready for use.

The relief of tears

All these are abnormalities, however touching and sad. The fact is that mourning is a necessity if grief is to be overcome. Tears are good, as a blessed relief. Any embarrassment of the sight of them, or any discouragement of them is much to be avoided, just as is revulsion at physical symptoms of illness. The Christian duty is clear. Paul set it down in Romans: 'Rejoice with those who rejoice, weep with those who weep'. (Romans 12.15).

Other reactions are to be expected. People who have suffered a bereavement seem at times to imagine that they are somehow to blame for the death which has taken place. If only they had done this, or not done or said that, or if only someone else had acted differently. The strange outburst of Mary after the death of Lazarus seems to echo this feeling: 'Oh sir, if you had only been here my brother would not have died'. (John 11.32). Just so may some widow bitterly regret a possibly unkind remark to her husband who shortly afterwards died, and blame herself for it. Such feelings may be emotional; but they are certainly real, and add to a sense of guilt hard to cure.

Blind anger

Anger, too, is to be expected — anger against God sometimes, and therefore prone to be directed upon those supposedly representing him. The parents of a dead child, for instance, can turn with much hostility upon the Parish Priest when he calls. Often this anger is a blind hitting out at anybody and anything, from the doctor supposed to have been at fault, to the would be comforter held to have said something false. Such anger needs to be understood, and endured by those trying to help. Even Job turned upon his friends: 'I have heard many such things: miserable comforters are you all. Shall windy words have an end. . .?' (Job 16.02).

A clergyman, in a remarkable letter to the press some time ago, wrote of this. He said: 'It is better for the bereaved to rant, rave and scream, even to go to church for the sole purpose of telling God how much they hate him, rather than bury anger and distress deep within themselves. Reserve and a stiff upper lip are not always the wisest things for mourners: they can turn inwards and develop long lasting depressions or great anxieties'.

Idealised image
There is also to be found in bereaved people the creation of an idealised image of the dead. They could do no wrong; they had qualities beyond compare; kind, loving, noble. This build up of the character of a person who may well in life have been ordinary enough — though none the less dear — can almost amount to the creation of an idol enthroned in memory. Once again Queen Victoria provides an instance. Albert, the perfect, became almost a deity, to the worship of which she devoted years of her life, remaining meanwhile withdrawn from the world. There are Victorias and Alberts now, in sad abundance.

Depressions, loneliness, feelings of insecurity are likewise to be encountererd in this shadowed country. Everyone who has loved and lost must expect to spend some time there. But not too long. There must, if life is to be renewed, come the time of an emergence again. How long bereavement lasts will obviously vary greatly from person to person. Bereaved people sometimes seem to know in their hearts when a true 'break away' moment has come, and they feel released from the prison of their grief.

Nobody can live in emotional solitary confinement forever, even when the cell is self made and adorned with an image of the deceased. Life must go on, and the choice is always between going with it or being left behind. But, blessedly, for the Christian with a strong sense of the timeless bond which unites living and dead, this never need or should involve any dwindling of the hope of meeting again.

Prayer
The continuing link between the two worlds of the living and the dead is prayer. It can be rewarding indeed to give imaginative thought to its best use. A man who had lost a young wife drew much comfort from setting aside each anniversary of their wedding and of her birthday for special commemoration, beginning with a Communion at which he both knew and felt he was meeting with her. Age cannot wither nor

custom stale such lovely acts. It does no violence to Paul's phrase: 'I thank my God in all my remembrance of you' (Philippians 1.3), to remember that it can be used for the dead as well as for the living.

Everyone's concern

The major question facing those who seek to help the bereaved is how best they may do so. Someone's loss really should be everyone's concern. In past times, and in small communities, especially villages, community support found expression in ritual. The ancient practice of a 'wake' is one example. These *rites de passage* as they have been called, are enormously important. The trouble is that in great impersonal city communities they don't seem to exist. Too many people have to face their bereavement alone. God alone knows how awful bereavement can be on great housing estates or inner cities or self exclusive suburbs where a sense of community simply does not exist. Too often there is only the doctor's surgery left, with some pills as the substitute for the love and support which friends could give. And alcohol, a potent drug indeed, can be far more dangerous because more easily available and less controlled.

Fortunately, considerable thought has in

recent years been given to this problem. People should not be left alone in their bereavement and it is a great help to enable them to share it. That is why to visit the bereaved, even when at first they don't appear to welcome the visit, is an immensely valuable thing to do.

It is often, with most people, in the two or three weeks after the funeral that grief strikes hardest. The 'excitement' is over; the need to show public composure is no longer there; those who came together for the occasion and maybe stayed on awhile, have gone. Then comes a time for the noticeable silences in the house which once held another voice: then comes the time for the sitting alone in front of the television. That is the time, beyond any other, for the helpful friend to be around.

Patient listener
To do what? Firstly to be there. Secondly to be imaginative of the needs of the bereaved to pour out at will emotions which have been damned up hitherto: of guilt, of grief, of helplessness. Thirdly, to be a patient listener to it all, knowing that by doing so far more healing work can be done than by any other means. Fourthly, to be one who recognises that the bereaved person has a work of mourning to do, and needs to be helped to express it, not to suppress it.

15

Above all, it is vital to tread delicately in the area of any overt attempts at spiritual consolation. A mother, made hypersensitive by grief, can be stricken rather than comforted by being told that her child is 'in Heaven', if only because the thought makes him seem further away, not near. To urge a bereaved person to 'bear up' is not helpful, either. Nor is any attempt to persuade them to look upon what has happened as 'a happy release'. It is not a happy release—for them. And though it may seem natural to urge cheerfulness upon the sorrowful, it can in fact be very much the wrong approach.

Unique event
The bereaved need their sorrow, and to mask it can only too easily come to seem a betrayal of the dead. Similarly, any attempt to diminish the experience they are going through by being philosophic about it — 'It happens to everyone, you know', can be hurtful. Bereavement for the person concerned is a unique event, and it is no more a comfort for them to be reminded that it is a universal experience than it is for someone in severe pain to be told that many others suffer it, too.

The way of the comforter is not all difficulty. There is much quiet satisfaction from realising how greatly simple yet imaginative acts of practical sympathy can help. Maybe it can all be summed up by saying that the secret of the comforter is love, which 'bears all things, believes all things, hopes all things, endures all things'. The reward for the comforter may be to become unneccessary when, in God's good time, the bereaved may have emerged from the Valley of the Shadow in such a sound emotional state as to be able to face up to the next task which awaits them, that of making out of their situation a creative bereavement.

Creative bereavement

'Many people misjudge the permanent effect of sorrow and their capacity to live in the past', wrote Ivy Compton Burnett in *Mother and Son*. Sorrow cannot be indefinitely prolonged, and the past is no place to linger when the future is possible. It has been well said that 'the melody that the loved one played upon the piano of your life will never be quite the same again; but we must not close the keyboard and allow the instrument to gather dust. We must seek out other artists of the spirit, new friends who will gradually help us to find the road to life again, who will walk that road with us'.

But for the Christian there need be no fear that in thus venturing into new paths the

departed will be, as it were, left behind until
with time they are out of sight and mind. The
practice of the faith, with its constant reminder
of the thinness of that veil which separates the
living from the dead, with the strong promises
of the Scriptures and the hope of the
Resurrection, is proof against that, if it is
accepted with conviction and with a resolution
to continue in it.

But it is well to give specific form to the
expression of this in relation to the dead. Not for
nothing was the custom of the early Christians
to remember them particularly at the altar. The
man mentioned earlier who in that way
commemorated at Communion the anniversary
of his dead wife's birthday and of their wedding
was on the right lines. Such acts do more than
give form and substance to a generalised hope.
They bring the living and the dead closer than
they are ever likely to be anywhere else in this
world.

THE LIFE OF THE WORLD TO COME

But however we manage to face up to our
bereavement, or to help others to face up to
theirs, with whatever courage, with whatever
determination, in the end there must always
remain the question as to whether we shall meet
again with our loved ones. This is where faith in

the Christian hope of the life of the world to come enters very much into the picture. Given this hope — and it can be ours because God gives it us — bereavement can be faced and lived through far more richly. 'Faith is the assurance of things hoped for, the conviction of things not seen' (Hebrews 11.1). What are these things hoped for? What are these things not seen? They are all the yearnings which press in upon the bereaved to meet again with those whom they have lost and who, for the moment, are not seen.

Jesus the conqueror
What men and women have always wanted to know about the departed — and about themselves when they join them — is whether they are utterly obliterated when their physical bodies are worn out or destroyed by sickness or accident, or whether they have some continuing existence. For the Christian, the hope of that is based upon Jesus, the conqueror of death and opener of the way to eternal life.

Jesus and eternal life
How did Jesus himself think of God? He thought of him as a father. He called him 'Abba, Father', and it is to him that he cries out in the Garden of Gethsemane before his death. (Mark 14.36).

There is a passage in Paul's letter to the Christians in Galatia which brings this out. 'To prove that you are sons God has sent into our hearts the spirit of his son, crying 'Abba!, Father'!'

Jesus never questioned the reality of the life of the world to come. He never argued for its existence. He accepted it as a fact. Jesus comes through the Gospels as one who was himself life. As he is depicted in St John he is from the beginning of things: 'All that came to be was alive with his life, and that life was the light of men. The light shines on in the dark, and the darkness has never quenched it'. (John 1.4). He is the master of all life and gives it in abundance. 'I have come that men may have life, and may have it in all its fulness'. (John 10.10). 'I am the way; I am the truth and I am life' he says in answer to a troubled question of his disciple, Thomas. He says of himself, too, 'I am the resurrection, and I am life. If a man has faith in me, even though he die, he shall come to life; and no one who is alive and has faith shall ever die'. (John 14.25).

Life and death
These are loaded and mysterious words. They are loaded with many layers of meaning, and they are mysterious because no one has ever

understood them fully or, maybe, could hope to in this life. What matters is the continual thread running through them indicative of the fact that Jesus has something tremendous and momentous to say about life in its relation to death. The main burden of the message is that he, who is life, offers those who choose to follow him a share in this destiny, and with others the promise of his companionship.

Eternal life

The message is to those who believe in Jesus, who accept him as Lord, and who choose to try as best they may to follow him. What Jesus asks of them, when he thus calls them to follow him wherever the way may lead, even through suffering and death, he himself does first. Freely, and because of love for the Father and for his own followers, he gives his life as the good shepherd lays down his life for the sheep. (John 10.11). But he thus gives his life in order to take it up again (John 10.17). Afterwards he becomes 'A life-giving spirit' (1 Cor 15.45), as Paul says, capable of bestowing the gift of life on all who believe in him.

But what kind of life are we talking about? When death moves people to hope about a continuation of the life of someone they have loved, stirring the expectation of meeting them again, it is natural enough to think in this way. But this is not the Christian hope. When Jesus spoke of life he meant eternal life, which is something quite distinct from any idea of existence as we know it continuing for ever. Eternal life is fulness of life which begins here and now as a Christian comes through belief in Christ, to be accepted by him through love for him. And though physical death is a stage along the path of life, for the Christian as for anyone else, it is only a stage. Death is absorbed by life. Indeed, the fulness of eternal life cannot be achieved without passing through death. What is mortal must be cast off, with all its limitations of time and decay, 'So that our mortal part may be absorbed to life immortal', as Paul puts it. (2 Cor 5.4). It is a lovely thought to bear in mind when we are faced with a bereavement.

Christian hope
Eternal life, indeed, 'We are in him who is real, since we are in his son Jesus Christ. This is a true God, this is eternal life', (John 5.20). So the Christian hope of the life of the world to come means far more than a generalised hope of immortality for all. It is not just a wish fulfilment. The Christian hope is based upon a belief in a person, and upon an event which happened to that person — the resurrection of

Jesus. And also it requires a response to that person, in belief and in service before it becomes real. The background to this reality, the documentary evidence for it, is in the New Testament.

The Resurrection of Jesus

This is the key to the whole matter. The Gospels are focussed more on the death and resurrection of Jesus than upon anything else. All that goes before leads up to this tremendous happening. Jesus died in the full physical sense. It was a dead man whose body was taken away for burial after the Crucifixion. It was a living man, albeit clothed in a resurrection body, who returned first to astonish and then to overjoy his Disciples. He had come through death. No one saw the happening. The actual resurrection is the great unseen event of the New Testament, just as it was also the great unexpected event.

But it was the good news of the Gospel: it became the centre of the Apostles' teaching from the earliest days of the faith. They knew it had happened. They believed as they came to ponder the mystery that it was a fulfilment of scriptural prophecy. But, above all, they found in it, as we may now, a dazzling hope of eternal destiny. Christ is in person the resurrection and the life. 'He who believes in me, though he die, yet shall he live, and whoever lives and believes in me shall never die'. (John 11.25).

We will 'rise' because Christ has risen. 'If the spirit of him who raised Jesus from the dead dwells in you, he who raised Jesus from the dead will give life to your mortal bodies also through his spirit which dwells in you.' (Romans 8.11).

The resurrection was real indeed to those who met Jesus afterwards and believed. They were chosen witnesses. Crowds saw him die; only a few saw him afterwards. Maybe here there is an analogy with the many to whom all this does not make sense, until they need it terribly, and the few to whom it is the word of life. Precious then is that word to those involved with the loss and sorrow which death brings. To the bereaved this hope is of the very essence of comfort and strength.

A timely text
There is one very specific statement of Jesus about the life of the world to come which rewards reverent examination because it has meant so much to so many so often. 'Set your troubled hearts at rest. Trust in God always; trust also in me. There are many dwelling places in my Father's house; if it were not so I should have told you; for I am going there on purpose

24

to prepare a place for you.' (John 14.1,2).
What did Jesus mean? Many have answered
this in various ways. George McLeod found
much illumination of this text in the fact that, in
the ancient world, caravanserais, staging points
for caravans, were built to offer security to
travellers when night fell. The messenger would
customarily be sent ahead to prepare places.
The picture sheds a small, homely light upon a
great mystery. Jesus has indeed gone before us
to prepare a place for us and for our loved ones.

How are the dead 'raised'?

There is one ever recurring question about death
and what lies beyond. If the dead are indeed
'raised'; if people enter after death upon a new
stage of being, what kind of body do they have?
This is a question very old and ever new. People
ask it today. Christians in Corinth in the first
century put it to Paul. For answer, he draws
upon the picture of the seed and that which
grows from it. It has to die, he reminds them,
before anything can come of it: 'What you sow
is not the body which is to be, but a bare kernel,
perhaps of wheat or of some other grain'. He is
speaking of our physical bodies which,
obviously, will at death perish. But then he goes
on: 'What is sown is perishable, what is raised
is imperishable. It is sown in dishonour. It is

raised in glory. It is sown in weakness, it is raised in power, it is sown a physical body. It is raised a spiritual body'. (1 Cor 15.42,44). And then he moves on to that terrific passage which echoes down the centuries: when the perishable puts on the imperishable, and the mortal puts on immortality, then shall come to pass the saying that is written: 'Death is swallowed up in victory. O death, where is thy victory? O death, where is thy sting. Thanks be to God who gives us the victory, through our Lord Jesus Christ'.

What is to happen, however, in the life of the world to come to those who die believing none of these things or, more likely, knowing none of these things. The Christian needs to be humble here. It may be that, through the grace of God, he has been enabled to know something of the hope that is in Jesus. But it is not for him, nor for anyone else, to presume to judge even for a moment what the will of God is likely to be for this or that individual. The Bible has one great phrase never to be forgotten when the ultimate destiny of anyone who has died is dwelt upon: 'The souls of the righteous are in the hands of God'. If God is God, and if God is loving, then it is not to be thought of that he is going to throw anybody away. To quote William Barclay again, he said: 'I believe in the life to come, not because of the proofs of the philosophers, but because the whole teaching of the New Testament is based on the assumption that there is life after death'. And so anyone who is bereaved may, in their sorrow, while they yearn after those who have gone and hope for a time when in a new day they will meet again, remember some lovely words of Cardinal Newmans:

> And with the dawn those angel faces smile
> Whom I have loved long since, and lost
> awhile.

WORDS OF COMFORT

When in need of reassurance
God is our refuge and strength, a very present help in trouble. Therefore will we not fear though the earth should change, though the mountains shake in the heart of the sea; though its waters roar and foam, though the mountains tremble with its tumult. . . . The Lord of hosts is with us: the God of Jacob is our refuge.

Psalm 46.1,3,7

When in distress
Cast your burden on the Lord, and he will sustain you.

Psalm 55.22

When in need of strength

Have you not known? Have you not heard? The
Lord is the everlasting God, the creator of the
ends of the earth. He does not faint or grow
weary, his understanding is unsearchable. He
gives power to the faint, and to him who has no
might he increases strength. Even you that
shall faint and be weary, and young men shall
fall exhausted; but they who wait for the Lord
shall renew their strength, they shall mount up
with wings like eagles, they shall run and not be
weary, they shall walk and not faint

Isaiah 40. 28.31

When in fear

Life limited by death? Nonsense! That is a great
mistake. Death hardly counts; it is a mere
appearance; we already have eternal life and
that reflection should give us great tranquility,
as those who feel themselves to be eternal. Do
not therefore be afraid of death. It is the
flowering of life, the consummation of union
with God. . . . We must think of the dead as
alive and joyful and we must rejoice in their
happiness, remembering that we are in close
and constant communion with them, our life
only separated from theirs by the thinnest of
veils. We must remember that this does not
separate us either from God, our eternal joy,

who more than makes up all that we lack, or from the companionship of those who are with God in infinite time and space. Let us be brave and keep the eyes of our souls wide open to all these realities; let us see clearly around us those things which others only care to see dimly.

The Abbe Henri de Tourville
Letters of Direction

When thinking of the departed

Who has not someone loved and loving spirit waiting there, waiting for a blissful reunion, waiting to welcome the newly set free spirit to the joys of paradise? Most of us have surely more than one such gone before us whom we hope to meet. Some of these are already there, waiting for us, ready to welcome us, ready to make us feel as though we have come home, instead of gone into a strange land. . . . Then welcome death! Welcome solemn messenger from our dear and loving Lord? Thou comest to call us away to joy and peace untold. Thou art but as the narrow stream which parts us from our promised land. Thou art but as the little golden gate which opens into paradise.

Bishop Walsham How

When wondering about the life beyond
> My knowledge of that life is small,
> The eye of faith is dim;
> But t'is enough that Christ knows all,
> And I shall be with him.

Richard Baxter

A final thought for the bereaved
> I walked a mile with pleasure
> She chattered all the way,
> But left me none the wiser
> For all she had to say.
> I walked a mile with sorrow
> And ne'er a word said she,
> But oh, the things I learned from her,
> When sorrow walked with me!

PRAYERS OF COMFORT

Lord help me to realise that love does not cease when we die. Surely those I love who have died still go on loving me as they come to live more fully and deeply with God. Yet Lord, it is hard to understand, our immediate loss makes us grieve, and forget that because of our union with you we are never separated from those who love you.

Michael Hollings. The Shade of His Hand

Oh Heavenly Father, help us to entrust our loved ones to your care. When sorrow darkens our lives, teach us to look up to you, remembering the cloud of witnesses by which we are compassed about. And grant that we on earth, rejoicing ever in your presence, may share with them the rest and peace which your presence gives: through Jesus Christ our Lord.

Canadian Prayer Book

Oh Lord our God, from whom neither life nor death can separate those who trust in your love, and whose love holds in its embrace your children in this world and in the next: so unite us to yourself that in fellowship with you we may be always united to our loved ones whether here or there: give us courage, constancy, and hope: through him who died and was buried and rose again for us, Jesus Christ our Lord.

William Temple

Give me, for light, the sunshine of thy sorrow,
Give me, for shelter, the shadow of thy cross.
Give me to share the glory of thy morrow,
Gone from my heart the bitterness of loss.

Geoffrey Studdert Kennedy

Bring us, oh Lord God, at our last awakening into the house and gate of Heaven, to enter into that gate and dwell in that house, where there shall be no darkness nor dazzling: but one equal light: no noise nor silence, but one equal music: no fears nor hopes, but one equal possession; no end nor beginnings, but one equal eternity; in the habitation of thy glory and dominion, world without end.

John Donne

Suggestions for further reading:
Dying, by John Hinton (Penguin Books)
On Death and Dying, by Elizabeth Kubler-Ross. (Tavistock Publications)
Bereavement, by John Murray Parkes
Death and the Family, by Lily Pincus. (Faber and Faber)
Visiting the Sick, by Norman Autton. (Mowbray)

© A. R. Mowbray & Co. Ltd. 1981

ISBN 0 264 66727 1

First published 1981 by A. R. Mowbray & Co. Ltd.
Saint Thomas House, Becket Street, Oxford OX1 1SJ
Typeset by Seacourt Press Ltd. Oxford
Printed in Great Britain by David Green Printers Ltd.